# The Ball Python Manual

## FROM THE EXPERTS AT
## ADVANCED VIVARIUM SYSTEMS®

*By Philippe de Vosjoli*
*with Roger Klingenberg, DVM,*
*Tracy Barker, David Barker, and Alan Bosch*

THE HERPETOCULTURAL LIBRARY®
Advanced Vivarium Systems®
Irvine, California

June Kikuchi, *Chief Content Officer*
Jarelle S. Stein, *Editor*
Karen Julian, *Publishing Coordinator*
Jessica Jaensch, *Production Supervisor*
Leah Rosalez, *Production Coordinator*
Indexed by Melody Englund

Front cover photo by David Northcott; back cover photo courtesy of
www.grazianireptiles.com.
The additional photographs in this book are by David Barker, pp. 4,
6–8, 10–12, 22, 24 (bottom), 34, 35, 36 (bottom), 50, 59, 63, 65, 67,
69, 70, 79 (bottom); Bill Love, pp. 9, 25, 64; John Patton, p. 14;
Philippe de Vosjoli, pp. 16, 20, 21, 24 (top), 66; Sandmar Enterprises,
p. 17; Neodesha Plastics, p. 18; David Northcott, p. 32;
www.grazianireptiles.com, 40–43, 45–49, 51–54, 56, 57;
www.alanboschreptiles.com, p. 36 (top); Isabelle Francais, p. 60;
Chris Wood, p. 61; Roger Klingenberg, pp. 72–75, 79 (top).

LCCN: 96-183295
ISBN-10: 1-882770-72-2
ISBN-13: 978-1-882770-72-4

An Imprint of I-5 Press
A Division of I-5 Publishing, LLC
3 Burroughs
Irvine, CA 92618

We want to hear from you. What books would you like to see in the
future? Please feel free to write us with any comments on our AVS
books.

Printed and bound in China
15  14  13       7  8  9  10

# CONTENTS

# INTRODUCTION

The ball python is one of the most popular and widely sold snakes in the pet trade. In 1991, more than sixty-five thousand ball pythons were imported by the United States alone, and thousands more were imported by European countries, Canada, and Japan. In the past, gravid females were exported with the rest, resulting in the loss of thousands of eggs and many unhealthy females. However, during the past decade, exporters established programs for the captive hatching of ball python eggs, and as a result, more imported hatchlings are available, and more ball pythons are exported by the countries of origin. The ball python is the last inexpensive python available in the pet trade, and, consequently, one of the most appealing to pet store owners and first-time snake buyers.

The snakes also appeal to hobbyists for many other reasons. In addition to their incredibly diverse and attractive colors and patterns, they do not grow too large to maintain or become large enough to threaten humans or household pets. During handling, they are reluctant to bite, and they readily become tame.

A variant of "jungle" ball python.

On the other hand, ball pythons are highly exploited, not only by the pet trade but also in their countries of origin, where they are eaten and their skin is used as a source of leather. Unfortunately, their reproductive rate is much lower than that of some of the larger pythons. Their egg clutches tend to be small, and they tend to breed every two to three years in the wild, rather than every year. If the current level of capture and sale is to continue, wild populations require careful management, including captive incubation of eggs laid by collected females and restocking programs. To understand their plight from a herpetocultural perspective, simply consider that a ball python is likely to produce fewer offspring during a two-year period than a green tree python (*Morelia viridis*), a blood python (*Python curtus*), or a jungle carpet python (*Morelia spilota variegata*), all of which are sold at much higher prices.

Although ball pythons are among the most readily available and least expensive larger snakes sold, they are also some of the most challenging. Adults and subadults tend to harbor parasites and commonly arrive with various diseases, including stomatitis (mouth rot), respiratory disorders, and protozoan and bacterial infections. Most of these medical problems usually go unnoticed and unattended by pet store personnel and first-time buyers. In addition, many adult ball pythons are reluctant to feed in captivity.

The goal of this book is to provide useful, up-to-date information on the husbandry and propagation of this often misunderstood species, including tips on how to overcome problems related to feeding.

# CHAPTER 1

# GENERAL INFORMATION

## What's in a Name?

The scientific name of the ball python is *Python regius*, which translates to "royal python," the name often used for the species in Europe. The popular name ball python, although not as accurate, refers to the propensity of the species to coil into a tight ball when threatened.

## Distribution and Imports

The ball python is found in the grasslands of the Sudanese subprovince (west of the Nile); in southern Sudan, in the Bahrel Ghazal River and Nubia Mountains region (southern Kordofan); in West Africa from Senegal to Sierra Leone; and in the Ivory Cost and parts of Central Africa. Virtually all ball pythons sold in the reptile trade are imported from Togo and Ghana.

A "high yellow" albino ball python. The incredible breeding potential of ball pythons has secured them a lasting place in herpetoculture.

This ball python is representative of wild morphs imported from Ghana and Togo.

## Habitat

Ball pythons are primarily terrestrial snakes that inhabit open forests or savanna grasslands with low tree density and scattered rock outcroppings. They are not found in closed forests but are known to colonize heavily cleared and farmed grasslands. Reportedly, trappers have set fire to grasslands as a collection method.

## Size

Hatchlings range from 10-inch runts to large, 17-inch specimens. Adults typically range from 3 to 5 feet in length, though there are reports of wild individuals reaching more than 6 feet long.

## Growth Rate

Ball pythons that are captive-raised from hatchlings grow to more than 3 feet in length within three years. With an optimal feeding and maintenance regimen, some ball pythons reach sexual maturity within two-and-a-half to three-and-a-half years.

## Longevity

The natural life span of ball pythons ranks among the highest for snake species. It is reasonable to expect a captive-raised specimen to live twenty to thirty years. The longest-lived ball python on record lived forty-seven years. Renowned herpetologist Roger Conant purchased the specimen as a young adult male. The snake resided in the Philadelphia Zoo from April 26, 1945, to October 7, 1992.

# CHAPTER 2

# SELECTION

An imported adult ball python is not a good beginner's snake. Captive-hatched ball pythons, usually available in spring and summer, are a good choice for interested herpetoculturists (those who study and keep reptiles and amphibians). If purchasing your first snake, it is wiser to choose one of the many captive-bred colubrids (nonvenomous snakes such as corn snakes or kingsnakes) or another type of boa or python. The spotted python (*Antaresia maculosa*), now captive-bred in the United States, is another good choice for beginners.

Imported adult ball pythons are not a good choice for beginners because they tend to have difficulty acclimating to their new surroundings. Most beginning hobbyists become discouraged during the task of persuading imported adult ball pythons to feed, which can be an extremely tricky task. Imported adults also commonly harbor parasites, and many owners become discouraged during the course of parasite treatment or when treating associated problems, such as respiratory disorders, stomatitis, and enteric diseases (all too common in imported animals).

Due to their intensive care requirements, imported adult ball pythons do not make suitable pets for beginners.

When buying a ball python, the best choice is a captive-born hatchling.

## Selecting a Healthy Python

Captive-hatched juveniles are the best choice for most interested hobbyists, and imported juveniles are a close second. Select a specimen that has a rounded body and does not demonstrate pronounced backbone or rib definition. Check to be sure that the skin is relatively clear and free from superficial injuries.

Once you have found a python that interests you, ask to hold it. A healthy ball python should give a distinct impression of strength and good muscle tone. Newly imported ball pythons in good health usually have a strong tendency to adopt the tight defensive ball posture. Avoid animals that seem to be limp or have poor muscle tone. These are always clear indicators of poor health.

Next, perform the following steps to determine the animal's health:

1. With one hand, hold the snake behind its head while supporting its body on a table or using your arm to hold it

against your body. With the other hand, gently pull the skin underneath the lower jaw to open the mouth of the animal. Look for the presence of bubbly mucus, which is a sign of respiratory infection. Another technique is to gently press your thumb against the throat area while the snake's mouth is closed. If it has a respiratory infection, mucus will often emerge from the sides of the mouth or through the nostrils.

2. While you have the animal's mouth open, look for signs of stomatitis. When it is present, areas of the gums will be covered with caseous (cheesy-looking) matter. In some cases, red, raw, and injured areas will be evident. Avoid any animals with these symptoms.

3. While you have the animal in hand, make sure its eyes are clear. If the snake is in shed, both eyes should demonstrate equal levels of opacity (clouding).

4. Check the body for lumps. Check also for depressed areas along the backbone and for collapsed areas along the sides of the body—a sign of broken ribs. Avoid snakes with any of these symptoms.

5. Examine the belly area to be sure it is free of signs of infection, including raised ventral scales, stained scales, or damaged scales.

6. Examine the vent (opening to the cloaca). The anal scale should lie flat against the body and should be free

A close-up of the head of a healthy ball python.

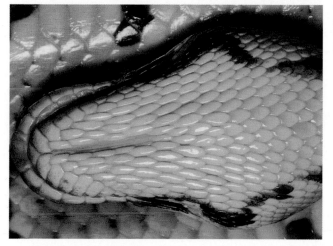

A close-up of the head of a healthy ball python.

of any caked or crusty matter. Avoid snakes that do not meet these requirements.

7. Look for ticks. These large, circular, and flat external parasites are harbored by virtually all imported ball pythons. If they are present, simply keep in mind that they will have to be removed when the animal gets home. Also check the animal for mites. These tiny, bead-like arthropods usually can be seen imbedded between the rim of the eye and the eye itself, giving a raised impression to the eye rim. Two reliable indicators of mites are the presence of scattered white flecks (mite feces) on the body of a snake and, following inspection of a snake, the presence of tiny mites crawling on your hands. Unless you are willing to deal with the treatment of these parasites, avoid mite-infested snakes. If you have other snakes in your collection, it is not a good idea to purchase snakes with these parasites. Be sure to wash your hands after handling the snake (a procedure you should always follow).

# CHAPTER 3

# QUARANTINE AND ACCLIMATION

I f you keep other reptiles, quarantine any newly purchased ball pythons in individual enclosures in a different room from where you currently maintain your collection. This procedure helps prevent the introduction and spread of diseases in an established collection. Standard protocol is to quarantine any newly obtained animal for sixty to ninety days prior to introducing it into any enclosure or room where established specimens are maintained.

Even specimens as healthy looking as this stunning morph must be quarantined and properly acclimated to their new surroundings.

## Acclimating Your New Snake

The following tips will help you acclimate your new ball python:

1. If you are serious about owning a ball python, have a good reptile veterinarian conduct a stool check on your new snake for parasites. All imported ball pythons tend to be infected with a number of parasites, which need to be treated. These parasites may include pentasomes, roundworms (nematodes), flukes (trematodes), and tapeworms (cestodes), as well as protozoans such as *Giardia* spp., *Trichomonas* spp., *entamoeba*, and *coccidia*. Ball pythons that have been treated for parasites are more likely to acclimate than those left untreated. The expense of veterinary treatment should be affordable to most buyers. If you cannot afford the cost of treatment, purchase a captive-bred ball python rather than an imported specimen.

2. Remove any ticks from your specimen by using a cotton swab to apply rubbing alcohol to the body of the tick. Wait a few minutes and then pull out the imbedded tick with a pair of tweezers. Make sure that you remove the entire tick.

3. Place the ball python in a suitable enclosure (see Housing and Maintenance) on newspaper. The heat in the enclosure should have a few gradients, including an area that reaches a surface temperature of 90–95° Fahrenheit (F). The enclosure should include a shelter and a large water bowl filled with clean, fresh water (refill it once a week or whenever it is fouled). Leave the animal alone for two weeks. During this time, do not handle it except to administer parasite treatment or to clean the cage (which will probably not be necessary during the first week). Check for mites, and proceed with treatment if necessary.

4. After the initial two-week adjustment period, assuming that the snake is not ready to go into shed (signaled by the dull appearance of the skin and clouding of the eyes), proceed with feeding (see Feeding).

A very large, imported female ball python. Use two hands when handling any large specimen.

## Don't Rush

Ball pythons require several weeks, sometimes even months, to acclimate to captivity. Once acclimated, animals feed with some regularity and thus gain and maintain weight. In time, they will tolerate varying amounts of handling.

## Proper Handling

When you first obtain a ball python, it will readily adopt a ball-like defensive posture whenever it feels threatened. Once it is in this position, allow it to remain as it is. Make no attempt to force it out of this posture except for necessary treatment and inspection. Most imported ball pythons perform this behavior and hide their heads rather than biting. Some specimens are more aggressive and will adopt the coiled neck and fore body posture that precedes a strike. When a ball python does strike, it usually consists of a quick strike-and-release sequence, resulting in superficial lacerations on the area of the bite. Once acclimated, and with occasional gentle handling, most ball pythons become quite tame and far less likely to adopt their characteristic defensive behavior. For obvious reasons, keep ball pythons away from your face during the initial handling and taming process.

# CHAPTER 4

# HOUSING AND MAINTENANCE

B all pythons require enclosures designed to house snakes securely. Suitable pens include commercial, all-glass enclosures with sliding-screen tops, commercial fiberglass enclosures with sliding-glass fronts, and custom-built wood or melamine-coated wood enclosures with front-opening glass or Plexiglas doors. Ball pythons are powerful snakes and notorious escape artists. Be a responsible herpetoculturist and buy a proper enclosure. If you use a hinged lid or door rather than a sliding top or front, be sure that the lid or door has a secure locking mechanism that prevents your snake from escaping. Cages such as all-glass aquaria with screened lids (usually sold for housing small mammals), are not escape-proof and are not specifically constructed for housing snakes.

## Size of Enclosure

The floor surface area of an enclosure meant to hold a juvenile ball python should be at least as large as that of a standard 10-gallon aquarium (20 inches long by 10 inches wide). This is the absolute minimum size you should use, and larger enclosures are recommended. For small adults, the floor area should be at least the size of a standard 20-gallon aquarium (24 inches long by 12 inches wide); a larger size is preferable. For very large adults, use an enclosure with a floor area of at least a standard 30-gallon aquarium (36 inches long by 12 inches wide).

A basic ball python setup using a commercial all-glass vivarium with sliding-screen top and locking pin.

## Substrates

Until a ball python is acclimated, the best substrate is newspaper or newsprint. It allows you to clean the cage easily and to readily monitor the condition of feces and certain aspects of maintenance (for example, the possible presence of mites). If mites are present, newspaper can be removed easily, thus providing the bare enclosure required for effective mite treatment.

Once the animal is acclimated, you can use a more decorative substrate. These include shredded cypress bark, pine shavings, aspen shavings, or medium-grade orchid bark (or fir bark chips). Take special precautions when using pine shavings: Be sure that no cedar shavings, which are toxic to snakes, are in the mix; and avoid pine shavings with a strong pine scent, as they are high in phenols and not recommended for use with snakes. When using aspen shavings, apply a thick layer and allow the snake time to

A melamine-coated wood enclosure with locking-glass front. These units are available with thermostat-controlled lighting and heating systems.

compress the shavings before its first feeding. If you use either pine or aspen shavings, inspect the snake's mouth area regularly to make sure that shavings have not become lodged in its mouth.

## Heating

Ball pythons require relatively high temperatures to fare well in captivity. In your snake's enclosure, the ambient daytime temperature should be 80–85° F. Your snake also needs a temperature gradient to thermoregulate. To create the gradient, heat one-third to one-fourth of the surface area of the enclosure to 90–95° F, which will serve as a basking area for the snake. The remainder of the enclosure should remain at the appropriate ambient temperature, depending on the time of day. At night, the ambient temperature can safely drop to a range of 75–80° F, as long as a heat source remains available for basking. During the winter, when conditioning the animals for breeding, lower the nighttime temperatures five to eight degrees to 70–75° F. (See Captive Reproduction).

Several heating systems for reptile enclosures are available in pet stores. Subtank heating pads and strips are the best ways to create a basking area and a heat gradient, and many high-quality systems are available. When selecting a heating system, consider the ability it gives you to control the temperature, particularly when considering heat strips and adhesive subtank heating pads. Without a temperature control, such as a rheostat, some heaters can become burning hot and can crack the bottoms of glass enclosures because of the extreme heat generated. If the substrate is flammable (such as pine shavings), an overly hot heater could set it on fire.

Some keepers use red incandescent light bulbs in fixtures with aluminum reflectors or ceramic infrared heaters to heat their ball pythons' enclosures. If you decide to use this method, use a thermometer to determine the appropriate wattage of the bulb for the space. Thermostatic controls are highly recommended.

Hot rocks are not a very good choice for ball pythons because the snakes tend to wrap around these heaters and burn themselves. Most commercial hot rocks are also too small and too hot. If you need to use a hot rock, buy one with a temperature control, and adjust the surface temperature with the help of a thermostat.

## Lighting

Lighting seems to be of relatively little importance to the health and maintenance of ball pythons. As long as all other conditions are met, including an available heat gradient, ball pythons will fare well even under low light. Many herpetoculturists interested in breeding ball pythons alter the photoperiod (amount of light and darkness) to

A 36-inch commercial snake enclosure ideal for a single ball python.

simulate long days during the summer months and short days during the winter months. Using timers, breeders typically set lights (usually fluorescent lights) to provide thirteen to fourteen hours of light each day during most of the year, then reducing this to ten to eleven hours each day during the winter cooling period. It has not been determined whether this plays a significant role in the breeding of species that live near the equator—and thus are exposed to more or less steady and equal daily periods of light and darkness throughout the year.

If you use incandescent light bulbs to heat a basking area, use red bulbs (available in large hardware stores, specialized lighting stores, and by mail order) rather than standard bulbs. Attach them to incandescent fixtures with aluminum reflectors and place them outside the enclosure, on or above the screen top. If you place an incandescent bulb inside an enclosure, it must be housed inside a wire mesh basket in order to prevent the possibility of thermal burns to your snake. Never place a bulb in an area that allows the animal to make direct contact with it.

## Fire Prevention

With any lighting system, take every precaution to prevent the possibility of fire. Use ceramic fixtures designed for the appropriate wattage. Never place heat-generating incandescent bulbs near or in contact with flammable materials. This includes curtains, wood, walls, and plastic wiring. Use surge-suppressor outlets, and always have a smoke detector in any room where you are keeping reptiles.

## Monitoring Equipment

### Thermometers

Monitor your ball python enclosures using a thermometer. Stores specializing in reptiles now sell inexpensive thermal-sensitive strips and other thermometers that work reasonably well for general purposes. For more exact readings, particularly if you are interested in breeding ball pythons, a digital-readout thermometer with an external probe is

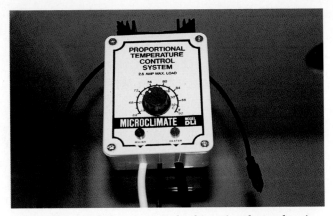

more efficient. If placed near a basking site, the probe gives a continuous readout of the high-end temperature in your enclosure. These thermometers also prove invaluable for monitoring incubating eggs.

### Thermostats

Thermostats provide an effective way to control the temperature in your ball python enclosures. Several types are currently marketed in the reptile trade, but only a few specialized pet stores stock them, so you will probably need to order them by mail through advertisements in publications such as *Reptiles* and *Reptiles USA*. There are two categories of thermostats: on/off thermostats, which turn a heating system on or off to maintain proper temperatures; and pulse-proportional thermostats, which essentially dim or reduce heat output to maintain a set temperature. The pulse-proportional thermostats allow for less temperature fluctuation than on/off thermostats and are highly effective for incubating eggs.

### Shelters

Provide a suitable shelter for all sizes of ball pythons. It should allow them to hide from the enclosure light and afford them a sense of security. Several suitable and attractive shelters, molded of plastic or concrete, are now sold in pet stores. As a temporary measure, use a cardboard box with a circular entryway for the snake. For imported ball pythons, use shelters with an opening at the top until they begin feeding (see Feeding). Attractive and natural-looking shelters can be made from large, curved sections of cork bark. Remember that a shelter is a necessary requirement for the successful maintenance of ball pythons.

## Suitable Shelters

Horizontal cork shelter

Vertical cork shelter

Clay shelter

# CHAPTER 5

# FEEDING AND HANDLING

**M**any newly purchased ball pythons refuse to feed, and this problem is the most common complaint of ball python owners to pet store retailers. It is also the primary reason that an adult ball python is not a good beginner's snake.

Remember, if you have selected a healthy ball python, it will be able to fast for several months without any ill effects. Reports of ball pythons fasting for up to a year before they begin feeding are fairly common. There are even two records of ball pythons that fasted for twenty-two months before feeding. So don't panic.

Imported pythons are kept in overcrowded conditions at various stages of their travels from their country of origin to animal dealers in the United States, exposing them to many parasites and diseases (often spread by infected sources of water). These factors directly contribute to a ball python's feeding impulse. Again, if you want to keep an imported ball python, have it checked out by a veterinarian and treated for parasites and diseases.

Coiling is a natural defensive reaction performed by ball pythons.

## Excessive Handling

The defensive coiling demonstrated by most imported ball pythons is a sign of stress, performed when they feel threatened. Many first-time snake owners are so charmed by their ball python's docility (it coils up in a ball or moves between the handler's hands without biting) that they fail to recognize their animal is, in fact, under stress. If your new ball python is active, it is probably trying to escape what it feels to be a threatening situation. If you are concerned that your ball python is not feeding, realize that stressed ball pythons usually do not feed. Therefore, you must stop handling the snake until it becomes accustomed to its captive environment. Unfortunately, most first-time ball python buyers seem to be overtaken by a compulsion to handle their new charge, which is very likely the primary cause of ball pythons' refusal to feed and thus indirectly a primary cause of death. To improve the survival chances of your snake, keep your hands off it and let it settle into its new environment.

### Hands Off!

Do not handle your ball python until it has fed at least four times in a row when offered food. After a ball python appears to be feeding regularly, limit your handling to a maximum of fifteen minutes per week. You can increase handling time after the snake has been feeding for three or four months. Stop handling it anytime it stops feeding.

## Feeding Hatchlings and Subadults

If you selected normal size captive-bred or imported hatchlings (15 inches and up), feeding is usually no problem. Hatchlings typically feed within a couple of weeks after their first shed, which usually occurs one to two weeks after they hatch. They normally feed readily on seven- to ten-day-old "fuzzy," or just-weaned, mice. It may be difficult to get runt ball pythons to start feeding and you may have to force-feed them pre-killed, five-day-old mice. Before resorting to force-feeding, offer food on several occasions for a period of up to four weeks after the first

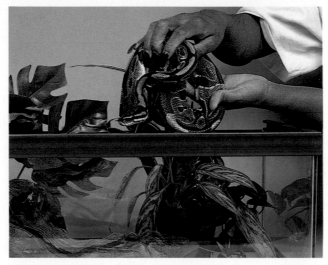

You can occasionally handle ball pythons for brief periods of time once they have acclimated and are feeding regularly.

shed. Force-feeding is always stressful, so do not resort to it until you have made a concerted effort to get a snake to feed on its own.

To force-feed a hatchling or juvenile ball python, gently grab the snake behind its head while keeping its body supported, either with your hand or with your arm against your body. With your other hand, insert a pre-killed mouse headfirst between the jaws of the snake using small, smooth, round-tipped forceps or straight hemostatic forceps (available through medical supply houses or specialized reptile dealers). Once the

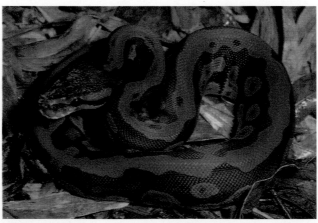

Captive-bred juveniles, like this wide-striped morph, rarely have the feeding difficulties associated with imported specimens.

mouse is between the jaws, gently push it past the python's throat area. Release the mouse and gently remove the forceps. Immediately thereafter, place the hatchling back in its cage and leave the area. If left undisturbed, hatchlings usually swallow force-fed prey inserted just past the throat.

Smaller ball pythons (less than 2 feet in length) typically begin feeding within a few weeks or months on mice, fuzzy rats, or weanling gerbils, which you should offer once or twice a week. As long as your snake's weight is adequate, there is no need to resort to force-feeding.

Offer food to hatchlings and subadults every five to seven days, and every seven to ten days to adults. Adults that show relatively little growth can be fed every two weeks. Hatchlings fare best on one food item of suitable size (the girth of the prey animal nearly equal to thickest girth of the snake). Adults will accept two or three prey items each feeding, such as adult mice or just-weaned rats, or a single larger meal, such as a small rat.

## Problem Snakes

Virtually every imported adult ball python sold in the pet trade has problems when it comes to feeding. When attempting to persuade a ball python to start feeding, first

Once you have some handling experience, it is easy to hold a snake behind the head, moving the thumb forward and pulling down the lower lip to enable examination of the mouth.

consider its feeding habits in the wild. Wild ball pythons are almost exclusively rodent eaters, feeding on several species of native African rodents, including various rats, gerbils, and jerboas. Wild ball pythons are primarily active at night and are considered active predators, investigating holes and rodent burrows for possible prey. They do not readily feed on mice or on the same species of rat normally offered to snakes, simply because these species are not found in their native habitats. Thus they need to learn to eat new prey with significantly different scents before they will begin feeding in captivity.

In the wild, ball pythons do not feed during the times of the year when night temperatures drop into the low 70s F or lower. Wild ball pythons tend to be inactive during December and January, when the sharp night temperature drops occur, and do not feed during this time. Breeding usually occurs following this period, and many ball pythons also will not eat during this period. After breeding, most gravid females do not feed. After laying the eggs, they brood their eggs, and do not feed during this period either, even though it may last for three months. Therefore, ball pythons have the ability to withstand long periods of fasting without ill effects. Imported ball pythons shipped between November and April may be influenced by internal and external factors that may cause them to enter a fasting period.

## Feeding Wild-Caught Adults

Remember to be patient and remain calm. Many wild-caught ball pythons imported between November and April may not feed until May or June.

### Standard Method

1. Allow a newly purchased ball python to acclimate for two to four weeks.
2. Provide the ball python with a shelter. Herpetoculturists recommend a shelter with an opening at the top (such as a large inverted clay flowerpot with an enlarged drainage hole) when feeding ball pythons. With this type of shel-

ter, the ball python stays isolated from any prey in its enclosure until it decides to emerge and capture the prey. Rodents that enter a snake's shelter elicit a defensive response in the snake and thereby discourage feeding.

3. Make sure that the ambient temperature in the enclosure is 85° F, with a 90–95° F basking area.
4. Be sure the ball python is not going into shed.
5. At night, introduce two fuzzy (unweaned) rats to the enclosure. If the snake doesn't eat them, repeat this procedure once each week at least two more times. If it still fails, try this technique again using an adult mouse. If this fails, offer a pre-killed gerbil. (Avoid using live adult gerbils. These animals can be aggressive and have been known to attack snakes.) Try this once a week for two more weeks. Switch back to a rat at least twice. Also try pre-killed, just-weaned rats. Switch back to a pre-killed gerbil. Try a live, unweaned gerbil and pre-killed adult mice.

If, after trying all of the above you are still without success, try one of the following methods:

## Brown Bag Method

1. Perforate a brown paper grocery bag a few times with a paper punch.
2. With the ambient temperature of the enclosure at 85–90° F, place the ball python and an almost-weaned rat (with its eyes still closed) inside the bag. Fold over the top of the bag, staple it shut, and leave it in the vivarium overnight. Check the next morning. If this method fails, repeat the procedure once a week for two more weeks. Then try the procedure with a barely weaned gerbil, or a pre-killed adult gerbil. Finally, try the procedure with a pre-killed mouse.
3. Repeat the entire procedure.

## Rodent Hole Method

1. This method is only suitable in large enclosures.
2. At night, place a small plastic bucket with a hole halfway up its side in the enclosure. The hole must be

just large enough to allow the snake to enter the bucket. Inside the bucket, place some shavings and rodent litter. Then add a fuzzy or nearly weaned rat, put a lid on the bucket, and leave it overnight. If this fails, repeat once a week for at least two weeks. If this method fails, repeat this procedure using an adult mouse or nearly weaned gerbil. If this attempt fails, repeat the procedure using a pre-killed rodent.

3. Repeat all steps of this method.

### Leaf- and Grass-Scent Method

1. Remove the ball python from its cage and place a layer of dry grass or leaf litter on the bottom of the enclosure.
2. Follow the steps listed above under "Standard Method."
3. Once the ball python has started feeding, at first replace only a portion of the grass/leaf litter with your personal selection of substrate. Gradually replace the remaining grass/leaf litter with new substrate.

If all of the above methods fail, keep trying. Usually, just as you are at your wit's end, you look into the enclosure one day and the rodent is gone. You cannot believe your eyes, so you search more thoroughly and then think, "Well, I'll be, how about that!"

Once a ball python begins feeding on any of the afore-mentioned prey items, you can offer larger prey as long as its size appears suitable for the size of your snake. You may also try to switch your ball python to a more readily available prey, such as small rats instead of gerbils. One method is to scent an alternative prey by maintaining it for one or two days in the soiled litter of the prey you are currently feeding your snake. Offer the litter-scented prey to the snake immediately upon removing it from the soiled litter.

### Force-Feeding

If treated for parasites and maintained under proper conditions, fasting ball pythons will not lose a great deal of weight, even after as long as a year. If, however, your animal is showing a marked loss of weight, attempt to force-feed it before its weight loss becomes too severe. Once an animal is emaciated and weak, the force-feeding procedure may cause enough additional stress to hasten its demise. Never let your snake reach that point.

Force-feeding is a stressful process. When a healthy and underweight ball python is picked up and handled for force-feeding, its natural tendency is to struggle, coil, and resist the process. Thus, force-feeding normally elicits a defensive reaction, which also means an increased tendency to regurgitate ingested prey.

## Force-Feeding Whole Prey

First kill a small fuzzy rat or a small adult mouse. To accomplish this in a quick and humane way, hold the rodent by the tail, and with a swift motion, strike the back of its head against the edge of a table. If you are in doubt, ask that your rodent supplier do this for you. After you have killed the rodent, lubricate it with water or a beaten whole egg.

Ask a friend to assist you. Remove the ball python from its cage and take it to a table or countertop. Next, take hold of the snake behind the head, gently yet firmly enough to hold its head still. Allow its body to rest on the table. If you prefer, stabilize the snake's body with your arm by holding the snake against your body. Ask your friend to hold the body. With your other hand, using large, round-tipped forceps, grasp the lubricated, pre-killed rodent behind the head and gently push it, head first, between the jaws of the ball python. You shouldn't have to apply much force during this process. A snake usually opens its mouth under these conditions.

Push the rodent in as far past the throat area as possible; the assistance of a friend can make this task a lot easier. Ball pythons tend to form a coil in the neck area that resists the passage of force-fed prey. At about one-tenth of the way down the snake's body, another coil also resists the passage of the prey. Once you push the rodent past the neck, release it and gently remove the forceps. Then, using your thumb against the ventral surface, try to push the prey about one-third of the way down the body length of the snake. Once again, do this very gently. After this procedure, immediately carry the animal to its cage, release it, and cover the enclosure so that it cannot see you or be disturbed in any way. In most cases, the snake will retain its force-fed prey. If it regurgitates, wait a couple of days and then repeat the process.

Force-feeding of any type is best performed by experienced keepers. During the course of any force-feeding attempt, you must be attentive to your snake's behavior. If you doubt your ability to perform this procedure, take your snake to a qualified reptile veterinarian.

## Force-Feeding a Liquefied Diet

A liquefied diet consists of three parts chicken baby food, one part whole egg, one-half part of either Pet Kalorie or Nutrical, and one part water. This mixture can be tube-fed using a large catheter tube attached to a syringe with a Luer tip, all of which can be purchased at a medical supply house. Lubricate the tube prior to use, and gently push it down the esophagus to just beyond one-forth of the snake's body length.

This procedure requires extreme care and is best performed by a reptile veterinarian or an experienced herpetoculturist (see Diseases and Disorders).

## It Ate!

Even after a ball python begins feeding, you can still expect periods of fasting. It usually takes several months before an imported adult ball python feeds on a regular schedule. It even may be necessary to repeat some of the techniques used to get it to start feeding. When dealing with ball pythons, patience and persistence pay off. If the snake has good body weight to begin with and has been treated for parasites, keep calm.

## Obesity

In captivity, overfeeding and lack of activity can cause ball pythons to become obese. Obesity increases the risk of disease, affects their ability to reproduce, and ultimately shortens their lives. The three observable symptoms of obesity in snakes are: stretched skin that causes exposure of skin between the scales, difficulty in forming coils, and fold lines in the skin from remaining in a coiled position for prolonged periods of time. When these symptoms are present, gradually cut back on the feeding schedule by decreasing the amount of food and/or feeding the snake less frequently. Once this has been accomplished, adjust the feeding schedule to maintain the animal's proper weight.

## Water

Ball pythons require a water container at all times. Use a container approximately the size of a medium-sized dog water dish, and fill it one-half to three-fourths full with clean water for drinking. A larger water bowl may help facilitate shedding when a snake is in shed, but a smaller container is best at other times because it discourages excessive soaking. Placing a water bowl partially over a heat source will result in increased relative humidity within the enclosure, which may be beneficial at certain times. Make sure the enclosure has adequate ventilation, so that condensed moisture does not accumulate. A damp cage encourages the growth of molds and provides a medium conducive to the bacterial infections that cause skin blister disease.

# CHAPTER 6

# BALL PYTHON MORPHS AND VARIATIONS

By Alan Bosch

D escribing the "normal" (wild type) ball python is difficult, as the pattern and color of this species vary considerably within a single clutch, let alone over its entire natural geographic range. To understand the color and pattern variations in the species, however, it is necessary to get an idea of what a typical, normally colored ball python looks like.

## Normal Ball Pythons
Essentially, the average ball python has a yellowish body with a dark back and a dark head. The head's color pattern is probably the most universal trait of ball pythons, which you'll notice as you study the many varieties. The eye is so dark that

Shown here is the normal (wild type) ball python.

the pupil is generally indistinguishable from the rest of the eye, and the dark line extending from above the end of the jaw through the dark eye to the nostrils further blurs the eye's outline. A pale line above and parallel to the dark line runs from the nape of the neck to the tip of the snout.

The rest of the body is covered in a series of dark blotches or vertical dark lines on the sides that may be partially fused into broken bands running down the back, quite often producing a dorsal stripe that continues to the tip of the tail. The dark blotches, lines, and bands are sometimes highlighted or edged with yellow or white. The sides show a lot of variation including no pattern, "alien heads" suggested by pairs of large dark spots ("eyes") within rounded pale areas, dots of various sizes, and darker side colors diffusing onto the belly.

The belly pattern is generally much lighter in color than the dorsal surfaces, being either a solid light color or a light color with some infusion of the side pattern's color. Speckling or blotching is often present, but the overall effect is always much lighter than the back coloration.

Ball pythons hatch out weighing between 1.2 and 3.8 ounces (35 and 108 grams) and are between 12 and 18 inches (30 and 46 cm) long at birth; they generally reach adult lengths of between 4 and 5 feet (1.2 and 1.5 meters). The largest documented ball python I have seen was a 6-foot, 3-inch (1.9-m) wild Ghanaian female found coiled around sixteen eggs.

## Predicting the Results

To better understand how breeders can accurately predict the results of breeding snakes together, it is important to have a basic understanding of genetics. The following is a simple discussion and is not intended to do more than give an overview of the principles and terms of the science of genetics, but it should suffice for our purposes.

### Genetics

Genetics is the science of heredity—why a plant or animal looks the way it does. The term *trait* refers to a quality or distinguishing feature such as height, length, color, or pattern. Traits are the expression of the genes stored in chromosomes, the bits of genetic material found in the nucleus of every cell in a living organism. Genetics studies the effects of the actions of genes and applies to all animals and plants, from bacteria to ball pythons to humans. With a basic understanding of genetics and how the mechanisms of genetics operate, many of the traits reptile breeders are interested in are easy to understand and consistently reproduce.

## Recessive Traits

Traits involving pattern and color are the results of the effects of either a dominant gene or a recessive gene. Genes for a trait are inherited from each parent. When they are combined (such as a dominant gene from the mother and a recessive gene from the father), the trait expressed by the dominant gene dominates (hides) the recessive gene's trait. When a recessive gene is combined with another recessive gene, the recessive trait is expressed; that is, it becomes visible. For instance, if an albino ball python (albinism is a recessive trait) breeds with a normal ball python (a dominant trait), all of the babies of this first (F1) generation would look normal because the albino color trait is dominated by the normal color trait (dominant gene from

Albinism, a simple recessive mutation, results in a snake lacking the dark pigment seen in the normal type. This fine specimen is a high-yellow albino, its yellow pigment being deeper and brighter than typical albinos display.

one parent, recessive from the other). In other words, all of the resultant babies are carrying the albino trait but do not express the trait since the normal color is dominant. However, if two of the resultant F1 offspring mate, producing the second (F2) generation, one out of four F2 babies will be albino because it will have an albino gene inherited from both parents in its genetic makeup. Below are some of the most common simple recessive traits:

- **Albinism:** Albino specimens have an inability to produce or use the tyrosinase enzyme that stimulates the melanophores to produce melanin (dark pigment); the trait is also known as amelanism.
- **Axanthism:** Axanthic specimens have an inability to produce or use the enzyme that stimulates the xanthophores to produce red and yellow pigments.
- **Piebaldism:** In most animals, piebaldism produces a dark spotted or mottled pattern on a pale background. It is somewhat different in the ball python: the head displays the normal type color and pattern, but the body has a pure white background with "islands" of normal color with an abnormal dorsal pattern. The exact chemical and genetic mechanisms governing the percentage of white, the dorsal pattern, and the placement of the

An axanthic ball python.

Dubbed Snowflake by its breeder Alan Bosch, this specimen is a high white piebald. Generally, piebaldism results in blotches of the normal color along the back as well, though the amount of color varies from snake to snake.

dorsal pattern are unknown. Details of the piebald pattern vary considerably from snake to snake and from clutch to clutch.

- **Hypomelanism (ghost):** This trait reduces the intensity of the dark pigments within the melanophores, producing normal pattern elements that are faded and have a satiny greenish, yellowish, or orangish appearance. Some physiological factors affecting the pigment cells (shape and texture of the scales, for instance) may play a role in this condition in addition to the actual genetics.

Ball pythons may carry recessive genes for more than one trait. For instance, a snake may carry the gene for albinism

A "high gold" and an axanthic ball python.

and the gene for piebaldism, but it will not show either trait in the F1 generation since both are recessive traits.

Some combinations of the base morphs (which we'll discuss a bit later) will produce predictable results. This is especially easy to illustrate with a simple recessive trait such as albinism. The first of the two following Punnett square diagrams shows that when two het albinos mate, one-fourth of the offspring will be albino, three-fourths will be normal looking, though two of these three will carry the trait for albinism. The second Punnett square shows that when two piebalds mate, all of the offspring will be pieds (again, recessive genes from both parents) and so on. Such snakes are said to be homozygous for a trait, meaning they are carrying a pair of similar genes—in this case both recessive—for a trait.

---

## Het Albino × Het Albino

**Possibilities:**
AA = normal
Aa = het albino
aa = albino

**Parents:**
Male = Aa, heterozygous
  (het) for albino
Female = Aa, heterozygous
  (het) for albino

**Male Parent**

|  | A | a |
|---|---|---|
| **A** | AA normal | Aa het albino |
| **a** | Aa het albino | aa albino |

(Female Parent)

**Offspring:**
3 normal-looking babies
  (two of which are hets, one is 67 percent possibly het for albinism)
1 albino

---

## Piebald × Piebald (Homozygous)

**Possibilities:**
PP = normal
Pp = het pied
pp = pied

**Parents:**
Male = pp, piebald or pied
Female = pp, piebald or pied

**Male Parent**

|  | p | p |
|---|---|---|
| **p** | pp pied | pp pied |
| **p** | pp pied | pp pied |

(Female Parent)

**Offspring:**
4 pied babies

Breeding two animals that carry the traits as recessives but do not express them becomes a bit trickier because the presence of these recessive traits can be determined only through breeding experiments or by knowing the parentage. For example, breeding an albino with a piebald (both simple recessive traits) produces F1 offspring that carry both the pied and the albino genes but do not express them (remember, each parent provides only one set of recessive genes for a trait, so a pair of genes for either trait is not present in the offspring), so the babies look normal (both parents provided a group of genes for normal appearance, thus this dominant trait will be expressed). Such snakes are said to be *heterozygous* (het) for both albinism and piebaldism, or in this case double hets, meaning they are carrying genes for two traits but not expressing them. Crossing the resultant *double hets* will produce, statistically speaking, a pied with no melanin (albino) in one of sixteen offspring. The Punnett square below shows this diagrammatically.

## Double Het Albino/Pied × Double Het Albino/Pied

**Parents:**
Male = PpAa, double het
Female = PpAa, double het

**Results:**
9 normal looking    3 pieds
3 albinos           1 albino pied

|        | PA | Pa | pA | pa |
|--------|----|----|----|----|
| **PA** | PPAA<br>normal | PPAa<br>het albino | PpAA<br>het pied | PpAa<br>double het |
| **Pa** | PPAa<br>het albino | PPaa<br>albino | PpAa<br>double het | Ppaa<br>albino het pied |
| **pA** | PpAA<br>het pied | PpAa<br>double het | ppAA<br>pied | ppAa<br>pied het albino |
| **pa** | PpAa<br>double het | Ppaa<br>albino het pied | ppAa<br>pied het albino | ppaa<br>albino pied |

As illustrated by this diagram, of the sixteen potential offspring, most (nine) of the snakes will look normal, three will be albino, three will be pied, and one will be an albino piebald. Wow—not a bad clutch! Most ball pythons do not produce this many eggs in a single clutch, however, so the desired result of producing an albino piebald may take two or more successive breedings to achieve. Ball pythons have low fecundity and produce small clutches of only about six eggs once a year. The statistical improbability that a highly desirable animal such as an albino pied will be produced from such a small clutch adds to the excitement and thrill of achieving it, as Ralph Davis of Ralph Davis Reptiles (http://www.ralphdavisreptiles.com) did in 2005.

Remember that each breeding and clutch represents an individual statistical throw of the dice—producing two clutches of eight eggs each does not necessarily give you sixteen chances of producing an albino piebald.

## Codominance

Some traits express themselves visually in the first genera-tion, even when heterozygous. When two of these visually distinct heterozygous offspring are bred together, a "super" version is produced. Essentially, a ball python morph is considered codominant when the homozygous form of the trait is visually different from that seen in the parents (which were heterozygous). Statistically, when a codomi-nant snake is bred to a normal snake, 50 percent of the off-spring will express the codominant trait. The first example of codominance in captive ball pythons was described in 1997 by Greg and Jacki Graziani of Graziani Reptiles (http://www.grazianireptiles.com) when they produced the pastel jungle ball python.

Here are some examples of codominant traits:
- **Pastel jungle:** The homozygous form is a super pastel jungle.
- **Yellowbelly:** The homozygous form is an ivory.
- **Spider:** Uncertain. This morph may not be a codomi-nant as this trait's genetics are still a mystery.

Codominant breedings have the added benefit of

producing a visual result during the F1 breeding, the "super" offspring appearing different from their parents.

## Unpredictable Results

In some cases, breeding two morphs together brings incredible surprises. In 2003, the Snake Keepers (Dan and Colette Sutherland, http://www.ballpython.com) bred two yellowbellies (unnamed at that time, the snakes were simply similar looking) together and produced the first super yellowbelly (ivory) ball pythons. The initial pairing was a product of the snakes looking similar, not because the genetics were understood and therefore the expected product of the breeding was unknown. Nice surprise, huh?

Greg and Jacki Graziani had a similar surprise when they bred a pastel jungle with a cinnamon pastel. They had predicted that the result would be a snake with a pattern similar to a pastel jungle, but with the orange or yellow highlighted or enhanced. Boy, did they get a surprise! The pewter pastel was the result, a snake with a similar pattern but with an absence of yellow and orange. Other breeders' additional breedings of unrelated snakes with pastel jungle and cinnamon pastel patterns have produced snakes that approximate their original intent, not pewters, thus indicating that more than one genetic factor may be influencing the final colors. Additionally, some of the offspring of

This super pastel jungle morph is a product of crossing two heterozygous pastel jungle parents.

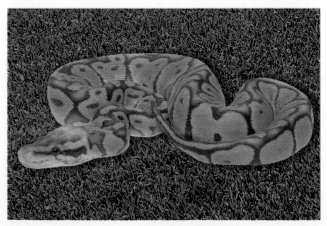

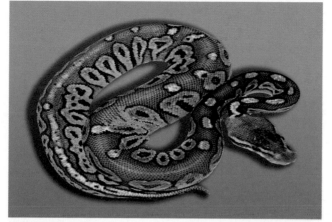

A surprise to breeders Greg and Jacki Graziani, this pewter pastel morph resulted from a cross of a pastel jungle with a cinnamon pastel.

the Grazianis' and other breeders' lines have evolved or metamorphosed as they aged, becoming yellow or orange. Only time and lots of notes and work will help us to unravel these mysteries.

Vin Russo (http://www.cuttingedgeherp.com) unintentionally produced the first blue-eyed leucistic. In 1999, a high-yellow (very bright yellow), wild-caught female purchased from New England Reptile Distributors (http://www.newenglandreptile.com) was bred to a normal male with the hope of enhancing the yellow in future generations. To Vin's wonderment, half of the babies looked like the mother. In 2002, he bred one of these high-yellow males to the mother and produced a blue-eyed leucistic.

## Pattern and Color Variations
The word *morph* is Greek and means "shape" or "form." The term is used to describe different colors, patterns, and body forms of animals, including ball pythons and other snakes, when they differ from the normal type, especially when they can be bred consistently in captivity. Although most snake enthusiasts consider ball pythons with normal pattern and color to be attractive in their own right, a lot of attention has been paid to the many morphs of the species. It is easy to understand why: these aberrant or unusual ball pythons are often spectacular and stunning at first glance, even more attractive upon close examination.

The stark yellow and white of an albino ball and the pure white and pied pattern of the piebald ball python stand out in sharp contrast to their litter mates with the darker, normal pattern. These morphs are easy to distinguish, yet other morphs have more subtle differences that at first may not be apparent to the untrained eye. But with practice and a developed skill to spot the abnormalities, you will notice these animals even after many people, including hard-core enthusiasts, have picked through them. I personally witnessed the discovery of a woma tiger ball, one of the most sought-after morphs, at a large reptile expo. The rare snake had apparently been overlooked by many pairs of eyes before someone saw and recognized it on a seller's table. These discoveries add an additional level of pleasure to an already exciting hobby, especially when the snake can be purchased for nearly the same price as a normally patterned ball python. I have personally found yellowbellies, granites, harlequins, and pastel jungles that the sellers simply labeled "nice," "odd," or "special" ball pythons and priced them only slightly higher than a normal ball.

## Morph Types

There are basically two types of morphs: base morphs and designer morphs. Base morphs are genetically repro-

A normal (above) ball python interlaces with an axanthic (below) specimen.

ducible types found naturally in the wild and in captive-bred snakes. Designer morphs are created by combining the base morphs to create rare pattern and color combinations. There are many base morphs currently recognized, and some are probably still to be discovered. For our discussion, we will focus on a few of the simpler, better-known base morphs and the designer animals that they can produce.

The red rat or corn snake (*Elaphe guttata*) should be mentioned here as a point of comparison when looking at the potential for morph possibilities in the ball python. The corn snake's morphs or aberrant forms have been reproduced successfully since the early 1960s, and its morphs are considered to be nearly limitless. The bases for these many morphs are really only albino, anerythristic (black albino), and a handful of other pattern types.

Many of the ball python base morphs, and some designer morphs, have actually been discovered in the wild. Many people wonder how animals that are so oddly or brightly colored survive in the wild when it is obvious that a predator would easily spot them. The fact that many morphs like albinos and pieds have been found as adults in the wild is probably a function of the natural living habits of the species. As a nocturnal predator, the ball python spends most of its active time moving in the relative safety of darkness, hiding in a burrow during the day. Much of its rodent prey is found and consumed at the end of an underground burrow where the ball python curls up and spends the next few days or so digesting its meal. The time that a ball python actually exposes itself to danger in the open where oddly patterned or brightly colored bodies would work against it is minimal compared with diurnal creatures.

## Base Morphs

The following chart includes the most common base morphs, as well as a few others of interest here. They are listed in order of the year they were proven to be genetically distinct.

| Year Proven | Base Morph(s) |
| --- | --- |
| 1992 | albino (also called amelanistic and T-negative albino) |
| 1994 | ghost (also called hypomelanistic) |
| 1996 | caramel (also called T-positive albino) |
| 1997 | axanthic<br>pastel jungle<br>piebald |
| 1998 | woma tiger<br>yellowbelly (also called heterozygous ivory) |
| 1999 | clown<br>spider |
| 2000 | Mojave |
| 2001 | lavender albino<br>pinstripe<br>platinum |
| 2002 | cinnamon pastel (also called black pastel)<br>fire |

The pattern of the albino snake is consistent with the wild type's, but the lack of dark pigment makes the albino easily distinguishable.

## Albino or Amelanistic (T-negative Albino)

This is the most obvious albino ball python. It would be more accurate to call it amelanistic, referring to the lack of dark brown or black melanin pigment. Since the dark colors produced by the melanin are absent, the underlying colors of white and yellow or orange become dominant because they are not hidden by the melanin. This type of albino is also called tyrosinase-negative (T-) because it does not produce tyrosinase, an enzyme that catalyzes the conversion of tyrosine into melanin by the melanophores, special pigment-producing cells. The head, body, and ventral pattern is the same as the normal (wild type) ball python; the difference lies only with the coloration, the albino lacking the dark pigment seen in the normal ball. The eye color is red and the tongue is pink, whereas both are very dark to black in the wild type.

## Ghost or Hypomelanistic

In this morph, unknown factors create a ghostly appearance in which the dark parts of the pattern are very pale. This is referred to as a hypomelanistic condition ("hypo" meaning below or under the normal amount of melanic pigment); hypo is a common abbreviation. The condition may be caused by a combination of chemical and mechanical agents acting together. The overall effect is a paling or lightening of the base hues and colors. It is commonly

The reduced amount of dark pigment in the hypomelanistic ball python gives this snake its ghostly appearance.

described as occurring in four basic types: yellow, orange, butterscotch, and green. The head, eyes, tongue, and pattern of a ghost ball python are all normal except for the pale appearance of normally dark areas. The shed skin of a true ghost will have no pattern in it. There are phantom ghosts that appear to be hypomelanistic but never produce hypo offspring. Their sheds have a pattern.

## Caramel (T-positive Albino)

In the caramel morph, some melanin may be produced by the melanophores, but not the normal amount. Unlike the

The caramel ball python gets its name from its light coffee-colored appearance, a result of the blending of the yellow and black pigments.

T-negative albino (T-), which completely lacks dark pigment, the T-positive albino (T+) displays a light brown pigment, which is created by a blending of yellow pigment with the melanin-produced black pigment. The enzyme tyrosinase is present and can be detected by simple chemical tests. The patterns on the head and other parts of the body are normal except for the caramel coloration.

## Axanthic

Their name meaning "without xanthins" (yellow and red pigments), axanthic ball pythons are generally black and white as hatchlings. Some specimens may appear to have

Axanthic ball pythons are generally black and white. Some specimens may appear to display light yellowish tones, but this coloration is a result of the way the snake's iridescent pigment-bearing cells reflect light.

some yellow, which is attributed to iridophores (iridescent pigment cells) that reflect light in a way that creates a yellowish appearance. This "yellow" coloration often darkens as the snake ages, indicating that the chromatophores are probably delayed in the production of yellow and red pigments. There is not a complete lack of these pigments. Tyrosinase controls the production of melanin and other pigments, and since it is normally active in these snakes at birth, it may have an effect on both the yellow and red pigment production as the snake ages. Time, good records, and lots of work will tell. The head and other aspects of the snake are all normal except as previously described.

## Pastel Jungle

This was the first ball python base morph produced in captivity that has both a pattern and a color scheme that are dramatically different from the condition in normal ball pythons. It is characterized by its odd, irregular pattern ("jungle") and pastel color scheme. Yellow and white are very evident and are more intense than in normal balls. The head is much lighter in color and often purplish compared with the normal type. The neck and body pattern is often aberrant, with wavy, squiggly, wormlike lines, sometimes with a much-admired purplish blush on the dorsal surface. The belly is always completely patternless and is usually white. The eye color is light, making the vertical pupil evident, and the tongue is pale.

## Piebald

The piebald ball python is one of the most distinctively colored animals in the world. The head and neck's somewhat normal to highly aberrant color contrast sharply with stark, pure white portions of the body, especially in snakes with a high percentage of white. Islands of normal color and pattern are scattered along the body and straddle the spine. Each island of color is generally distinguished by a pair of parallel dark stripes on either side of the spine on a brown, yellow, or orange background. The chin is odd in

With this bird's-eye view, we can see the characteristic sets of parallel lines that straddle the piebald ball python's spine.

that it usually is a smoky gray color that diffuses into the pure white of the belly by the time it reaches the throat. The head pattern and the eye and tongue coloration are normal. These are truly stunning snakes!

## Woma Tiger
This snake's appearance is most similar to that of the spider ball python (see following), although there is no known genetic link. The diffused color of the sides is not as strong as in the spider. In the woma tiger, the head has a light background with some orange hues. The eyes and tongue are pale. The neck pattern often is aberrant, and the back pattern is best described as a spiderlike reduced pattern without any conformation. The belly pattern is drastically reduced or may be absent. The tail is normal with a continuation of the back pattern.

## Yellowbelly
This is one of the true mystery snakes as it is difficult to recognize unless you can trace the parentage. Most of its external markers are variable at best. Generally, there is a light spot on the center of the top of the head that may be either quite visible or obscure. The eyes are dark as seen in the wild type ball, and the tongue is pale. The neck, back, and tail patterns are also normal, but some specimens have

The yellowbelly morph is one of the most difficult to identify, but look for yellowish tint on the belly as well as triangle-shaped color blotches jetting into the side pattern as seen in this specimen.

a brighter yellow color. Look at the ventral and side coloration for your confirmation: the yellowish or whitish patternless belly forms "triangles" of color intrusion into the side pattern, and a speckled appearance sometimes is apparent.

In order to determine if a snake that you suspect is a yellowbelly is indeed a yellowbelly, it must be bred to either another yellowbelly or to a normal snake. If a true yellowbelly is bred to a normal ball, approximately half of the babies will be yellowbellies. If two yellowbellies are bred together, then one out of four babies will be a super yellowbelly (ivory; see also the earlier section on codominance), also confirming the heritage.

### Clown

The original specimen from which Dave and Tracy Barker of Vida Preciosa International, Inc., (http://www.vpi.com) derived the clown name had a dark area like a "clown's tear" marking below its eye. This mark is sometimes evident but is not a necessary indicator. Pattern variation within this morph—even within a single clutch—is extreme, making a description difficult.

As a rule, the head is multicolored in light hues of brown, orange, and rust. The pattern is quite nondescript

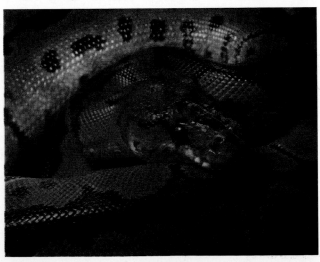

The clown morph's colored lateral blotches are extended and fused, resulting in an irregular mid-dorsal stripe that continues to the tail tip. This morph's name is attributed to the "clown's tear" facial marking, though it may be obscure or even absent in some specimens.

but generally includes a set of "spectacles," formed by the color of the lightest part of the body running between the eyes, down the nose, and then across the bridge end of the snout. The eyes are lighter than the normal type's, with the pupils evident. The tongue is pale. The neck shows the beginning of a dorsal stripe that often blends into the head color, and the back is covered by a dark dorsal stripe that sometimes melts slightly down the sides, which have a reduced pattern or sometimes no pattern; the end of the dorsal stripe goes to the tip of the tail. The belly is patternless and generally white.

## Spider

This stunning morph is characterized by a distinctive "webbed" pattern on the head and body with an unusual diffusion of yellow and white on the sides. The head has a light, rust-colored background interlaced with dark brown markings that form the "web." This pattern extends down the neck, along the back to the tail, and down the sides. The belly is usually pure white, but in some specimens is yellowish. On the back, the background color becomes a diffused mix of brilliant white from the belly and an intense yellow from the sides. The eyes and tongue are pale.

The weblike dorsal pattern on this spider ball python makes this morph one of the most desirable ball pythons.

The Mojave morph lacks the black, brown, and gold seen in the wild type. This specimen's beautiful dorsal pattern shows some unusual blushing in the dark bands that extend to the belly.

### Mojave

At first glance, many Mojave ball pythons possess a fairly normal pattern and color scheme, but further inspection reveals some distinct differences, especially in the color intensity and diffused back pattern. The body has a fairly standard coffee-colored pattern with extensive highlighting and light dorsal blotches, the pattern diffusing into a lighter coffee color as it blends with the belly. Dorsal blotches often end in a stripe continuing to the tail tip. The eyes are dark but with a somewhat evident pupil, and the tongue is pink.

### Lavender Albino

This albino morph's look is quite different from the amelanistic albino in a number of ways. The bright yellow blotches edged in pumpkin orange, the pearl white chin, and the lavender-bluish-white background color distinguish this snake from all other albinos. The pattern is otherwise the same as the standard amelanistic albino. It is a simple recessive form and has been used to produce some outstanding designer morphs.

### Pinstripe

There never is any doubt about what you are looking at when you see a pinstripe ball python morph. The head is

Two thin, black lines that border a lighter dorsal stripe create "pinstripes" along this ball python's spine.

light brown with dark eyes and a pale tongue, and the entire length of the neck, back, and tail has a light brown dorsal stripe with narrow dark borders (the pinstripes). There may be small offshoots of striping descending from the main dorsal stripe toward the clear belly and bordered with white flushes. This is truly an extraordinary ball python!

### Platinum

This is one of the most strikingly colored ball pythons due to its extreme hypomelanistic (hypo) coloration. The following is based on a description of the original male imported by Ralph Davis in 1999. The head is a light, goldish color with pale green eyes and a pale tongue. A light brown dorsal pattern begins at the neck, changing into an aberrant dorsal pattern of a stripe broken by a series of very light creamy blotches, and ending with a dorsal stripe that continues to the tip of the tail. The sides are nearly patternless, with a diffused mix of light creamy brown and beautiful white melting into the white, patternless belly.

The lesser platinum is the product of breeding the platinum to a wild type. A similar ball python morph, the butter, has yet to produce a blue eyed leucistic when bred to another butter morph.

This cinnamon pastel's lack of yellow pigment results in this morph's reddish appearance.

### Cinnamon Pastel (also Black Pastel)

The cinnamon pastel and black pastel morphs are essentially the same, so the following description applies to both. This is one of the base morphs with a patternless belly. The head has light upper labial (lip) scales and an eye band that is extremely reduced and pale tan. The top half of the eye's iris is silver and the bottom half is dark. The tongue is pale. The pattern on the neck, sides, and tail is fairly normal, with a dorsal stripe that runs from the neck to the tail. The color lacks the wild type's yellow, which gives the cinnamon pastel's its reddish appearance.

### Fire

The fire ball python is a brightly colored, pale yellow snake with a ghostly appearance, but the yellow is more intense than in the ghost morph. All other aspects of the pattern of the fire ball are normal.

## Designer Morphs

All of the designer morphs have been created by breeding together two of the base morphs or inbreeding a single morph, producing many new and exciting designer ball python colors and patterns. Most are codominants. Some are absolutely spectacular. Here are some of the most basic combinations and their results, arranged in order of the year they were developed.

| Year Developed | Combination | Results |
|---|---|---|
| 1999 | pastel jungle × pastel jungle | super pastel jungle |
| 2001 | pastel jungle × spider | bumble bee |
| 2001 | het albino × het axanthic | snowball |
| 2002 | fire × fire | black-eyed leucistic |
| 2002 | Mojave × lesser platinum | blue-eyed leucistic |
| 2002 | pastel spider × pastel spider | super pastel spider |
| 2003 | pastel jungle × spider | spinner |
| 2003 | yellowbelly × yellowbelly | ivory |
| 2004 | cinnamon pastel × cinnamon pastel | super cinnamon |
| 2004 | cinnamon pastel × pastel | pewter |
| 2005 | heterozygous lavender albino piebald × heterozygous lavender albino piebald | lavender albino piebald (LAP) |

## Super Pastel Jungle

This is essentially an extreme pastel jungle. The "super" displays greater blushing on the head and back, with the black and yellow coloring faded. Some describe the young as being very pale with an opalescent sheen. A beautiful snake!

## Bumble Bee

This sharp-looking cross of a spider with a pastel jungle results in the best of both snakes: the extreme weblike pattern of the spider contrasted strongly against the high yellow-orange of the pastel jungle. The yellow-orange color is especially intense on the dorsal surfaces and halfway down the sides with the lower half being white and the belly yellow. Quite often, the yellow-orange will outline the back webbing as it extends down the sides into the white background adding to the extreme look.

### Snowball
As the name implies, the snowball ball python should be snow white with no color or pattern. The eyes are brilliant red. Babies show very little or no pattern, though some light patterning may be evident as the snakes mature into adulthood. Selective breeding should produce pure white snowballs without pattern traces someday.

### Black-Eyed Leucistic
This is a pure white ball python with coal black eyes.

### Blue-Eyed Leucistic
These snow white ball pythons have cobalt blue eyes.

These blue-eyed leucistic ball pythons are the resulting offspring of crossing a Mojave with a lesser platinum. Other crossings have also produced blue-eyed leucistics, including Mojave × Mojave and lesser platinum × lesser platinum. A black-eyed version results from crossing two fire ball pythons.

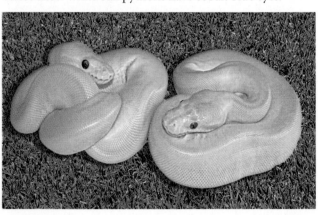

### Super Pastel Spider
Also known as the "killer bee spider," this is an outlandishly attractive snake with blackish purple banding, soft lemon-yellow background pigmentation, a white head with fine symmetrical patterning, and deep green eyes.

### Spinner
Combine the color of a pastel jungle with the pattern of a pinstripe and you get the spinner.

## Ivory

This ball python has blue eyes with red pupils. It has yellow dorsal striping bordered by a lavender tint on a white background. The yellow and lavender intensify as the snake matures.

## Super Cinnamon

This patternless black ball python with a white belly has great potential!

The gray chin of this super cinnamon morph shows the last hint of white from the belly coloration.

## Pewter

This designer morph has a pastel jungle pattern with no yellow at all and a pronounced, broad dorsal stripe. The snake has a metallic pewter-like look to it with peach or salmon colors on the sides.

## Lavender Albino Piebald (LAP)

A tremendously beautiful snake, it has all of the attributes of both the pied and the lavender albino morphs combined to produce a simply stunning ball python.

## Other Possibilities

Space limits our discussion to only a few of the more than one hundred base and designer morphs (according to John

Berry, author of *Investment Morphs*, www.johnberryreptiles.com). Mathematically, the combinations of these animals are mind boggling when multiple genetic traits are combined to create new designer morphs. The number of new and exciting marketable morphs is limited only by the breeder's imagination. Imagine, if you will, these combos and the possible outcomes:

- piebald × super cinnamon = salt and pepper, a pied snake with pure black saddles;
- piebald × spider = SpiBald , a pied with a spider saddle pattern;
- piebald × genetic stripe = striped pied, a pied body with a striped saddle pattern and light head color;
- double het genetic stripe/ghost × double het genetic stripe/ghost = striped ghost;
- granite × ivory = leopard, a white snake covered in dark speckles.

## The Future

It is obvious that the ball python is one of the most naturally diverse species of snakes. Compared with the average snake species, the ball python's potential for development of marketable morphs is astronomical—even when compared with the corn snake. The potential for the development of designer morphs promises huge opportunities for the average hobbyist or the serious collector and breeder to have more fun than a human being should be allowed—and offer the possibility a huge financial potential.

# CHAPTER 7

# CAPTIVE REPRODUCTION

By Tracy Barker and David Barker

S uccessful reproduction of captive ball pythons is fairly predictable. Many hobbyists have bred their captive ball pythons successfully, although most these breedings receive little notice. To date, the most prominent breeding success with this species has been with albino specimens. Many python breeders work with these animals, and their endeavors to establish a strain of albino ball pythons have resulted in three generations of captive albino ball pythons.

## Sexing

Both sexes of ball pythons have large cloacal spurs. In most adult specimens, the spurs of intact males are larger and have a more inward hook than the spurs of females. However, the spurs of older adult male ball pythons are often worn, their tips blunt and rounded, and sometimes they appear smaller than the spurs of a female of similar size.

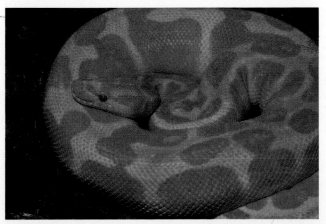

An albino ball python.

The most reliable way to sex adult ball pythons is to introduce a smooth, blunt, slender, and lubricated probe into the cloaca. By gently pushing the probe against the posterior wall of the cloaca, one can determine how far it can be pushed into the base of the tail. In males, the probe will pass deep into the tail without resistance, passing inside the inverted hemipenis, while in females, the probe will not reach as far. Thus, sex can be distinguished by the distance the probe can reach without resistance. A sexing probe will pass into the tail of a male ball python a distance of eight to ten subcaudal scales, while it typically reaches only two to four subcaudal scales in a female snake.

A breeder determines the sex of this male ball python using a sexing probe.

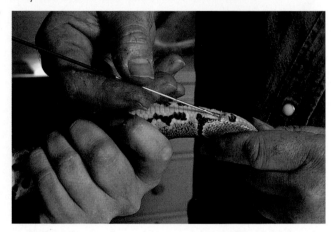

Ball pythons of any age can be sexed by probing the cloaca for the presence of hemipenes, but hatchlings can be easily sexed using a method known as "popping." To perform this method, place the thumb of one hand on the anal scale and use it to gently pull the scale forward, exposing and lightly opening the vent. Place the thumb of your other hand on the subcaudal surface of the base of the tail and, applying gentle pressure with a rocking motion toward the vent, attempt to evert the hemipenes of males. The hemipenes of hatchling males are small and have a visible red blood vessel on their medial surface.

Ball pythons can be reliably sexed using the popping method only during the first few weeks after hatching. After that time, young males gain sufficient muscle control

Vent area of male ball python.

of their hemipenes to render sex identification uncertain. Hatchling ball pythons are delicate, so it is critical to gently restrain them when sexing and to avoid subjecting their spine to excessive compression or stretching.

## Sexual Maturity

In order to breed, ball pythons must be old enough and large enough, but both factors vary from specimen to specimen. Because reproduction is strenuous and metabolically taxing for female ball pythons, overall health, condition, and weight are primary considerations. Responsible breeders carefully assess the condition of their animals, breeding them only if the snakes are in excellent overall physical condition.

Male ball pythons are likely to produce viable sperm by six months of age, but they should not be sexually active at that time. Males become predictable breeders at a weight of about 650 grams, usually at sixteen to eighteen months of age. Even so, the breeding attempts of young males may be tentative. Older males exceeding three years of age and 1,000 grams in weight tend to be the best breeders.

Females usually must weigh more than 1,000 grams to reproduce successfully. The first potential breeding season for most females is their third winter; at that time most females are twenty-seven to thirty-one months of age. There are records of ball python females producing fertile eggs after mating during their second winter, but this is rare and the few resulting clutches for which we have records are small, numbering between one and four eggs.

# Weight Gain in Female Ball Pythons

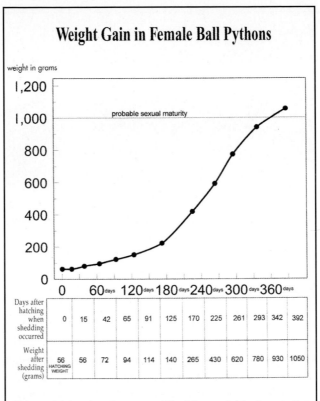

weight in grams

| Days after hatching when shedding occurred | 0 | 15 | 42 | 65 | 91 | 125 | 170 | 225 | 261 | 293 | 342 | 392 |
|---|---|---|---|---|---|---|---|---|---|---|---|---|
| Weight after shedding (grams) | 56 HATCHING WEIGHT | 56 | 72 | 94 | 114 | 140 | 265 | 430 | 620 | 780 | 930 | 1050 |

This graph is based on the average of the data recorded for three captive-bred female ball pythons. These animals were kept in optimum conditions, as evidenced by their rapid growth. The animals were weighed and the weight recorded after each shedding.

## Reproductive Longevity

Ball pythons have long reproductive lives and can reproduce through their twenties. A female ball python housed at the Saint Louis Zoo for thirty-two years laid a clutch of fertile eggs when she was thirty-five years old.

## Natural Reproductive Cycles

Ball pythons are nearly equatorial in distribution; most of the species' range is found between 5 and 15° north latitude. There is little variation in day length near the equator, and natural light cycles approximate twelve hours of light and twelve hours of dark throughout the year. Daily temperatures typically vary from 90 to 110° F during the warmest time of the year, and from 75 to 86° F during the coolest periods.

Wild ball pythons are seasonal breeders. The natural reproductive cycle of ball python populations in Ghana and Togo (where most captive specimens originated) appears to correlate with the two cool rainy periods that occur in normal years. Mating pairs of ball pythons are encountered most often from mid-September through mid-November. This period of time is known as the minor rainy season, a relatively cool couple of months, during which it rains almost every day. The dry season begins at the end of November, and the weather becomes progressively hotter and drier through March, the hottest month. Most ball python eggs are laid during the last half of the dry season, from mid-February to the beginning of April. The major rainy season usually begins in mid-April with several weeks of intermittent showers; April and May are hot and steamy, June and July begin to cool, the rains end in mid-July, and August typically is dry and is the coolest month of the year. Most ball python eggs hatch during the period from mid-April to mid-June.

A female ball python displaying maternal brooding of eggs.

## Captive Reproduction

Kept at constant temperatures and photoperiods throughout the year, captive ball pythons seldom produce fertile eggs, even though they may mate. In captivity, ball pythons usually require a change in environmental conditions to successfully reproduce. It is not necessary to reproduce the exact annual climatic patterns of West Africa in order to reproduce captive ball pythons, if such a feat has even been attempted. Breeders of ball pythons typically provide a gradually changing annual light cycle, varying from fifteen hours of light at summer solstice to nine hours of light at winter solstice.

We feed our pythons weekly throughout the fall in preparation for their winter fast. Many males and some females cease feeding at some point during this period as the days become shorter. For those animals that continue to feed, we stop feeding during the last week of November. Beginning in mid-December, we lower the ambient temperatures to daytime maximums of 82° F and nighttime minimums of 75° F. We maintain these ambient winter temperatures until the last week of February, at which time we resume the normal maintenance temperatures. We offer food to the snakes after this cool period, usually during the first week of March. On occasion, our ball

In captivity, ball pythons require a change in environmental conditions to successfully reproduce.

pythons have experienced temperatures as low as 61° F for overnight periods without apparent ill effects.

During the winter cooling period, we provide each ball python with a supplemental basking spot, providing a small area of warm temperatures of 85–90° F. Typically males and females spend little time basking during December and January. In February, they begin spending increasing amounts of time in these warm spots, usually basking several hours daily.

In late February, when the winter cooling period is discontinued, we continue to provide the basking spot, increasing the temperature and providing daily fluctuation of temperatures at the basking spot, from nighttime lows of 86° F to daytime highs of 95° F.

Usually, male ball pythons live together amicably, but during the winter, some male ball pythons enter combat. In general, the combat is harmless, consisting of much pushing and wrestling. The objective of each participant appears to be either to raise its head over the head of the other, or to push the head of the other to the ground with its body. Although biting is not normally a component of these battles, we have seen it in other python species. Therefore, watch any aggressive ball pythons to make certain that none of them resort to biting. When biting occurs

Ball pythons copulating.

as a part of male combat of other species of pythons, trauma can result, including deep wounds, eye injuries, skin tears, and death (though this is rare).

Combat often stimulates inactive male pythons to court and breed females placed in their cages. Many python breeders purposely place males together, encouraging combat between them, before placing the males with females for mating.

We place male and female ball pythons together in late December. A male can be placed with up to five females. In some cases, the pairs or groups remain together until late March, but we usually keep pairs together for three-day periods each week and then separate them and return them to their own cages. We normally place females in the males' cages, but placing males into the females' cages seems to work just as well.

Breeders often house captive-hatched ball pythons individually in plastic shoe boxes containing a small water dish. The box is placed on a shelf with heat tape on a rheostat running along one side. This housing method works for short-term keeping of large numbers of animals.

We observe two general periods of copulation, usually during the shortest day lengths and coolest temperatures in January, and again in March after the females have resumed feeding. Females typically ovulate during the period of mid-March through April, from six to thirty days after the last copulation.

Ovulation is clearly marked by a sudden large mid-body swelling. This swelling is created by the synchronous release of all follicles by both ovaries. Once released from the ovaries, the follicles are termed ova. The ova are pushed forward in the body cavity to the opening of each of the two oviducts, which lie anterior to the ovaries near the halfway point of the ball python's length. The ova are jammed together at the oviducts' openings by the muscular compression and tight coils of the body posterior to the swelling. Following ovulation and the mid-body swelling, the ova are taken into the oviduct and then passed through the oviduct. The mid-body swelling diminishes as all the ova are positioned along the lengths of the oviducts, where they are shelled, and the snake resumes relatively normal proportions and symmetry. The mid-body swelling in ball pythons lasts about twenty-four hours and is most apparent for about eight hours in the middle of that period.

About twenty days after ovulation, female ball pythons begin a shed cycle. During this period, many females continue to eat, while others cease feeding after ovulation. They lay eggs between twenty-four and thirty-four days after shedding their skin. Females do not normally eat during the period between the shed and egg laying, and we recommend that you do not feed gravid females during this four-week period.

Egg laying usually occurs at night; females are typically found coiled around their eggs in the morning. If allowed, females will coil around their clutches until hatching. We have not seen muscular twitching or shivering in brooding

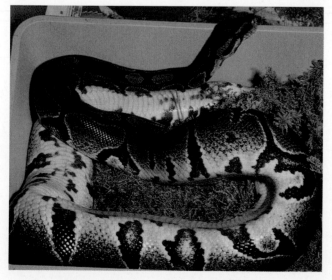

A gravid female ball python.

female ball pythons, or other evidence that this species is able to raise its body temperature metabolically while brooding, which we have observed in several other python species. Brooding female ball pythons sometimes leave their clutch to bask, and they may drink and feed during these brief periods away from their eggs.

## Reproductive Effort
A clutch of ball python eggs commonly represents a significant percentage of the female's weight, ranging from 17 to 65 percent. The average ratio in eighteen clutches was nearly 47 percent.

## Eggs
Ball python eggs measure 71–96 millimeters (mm) in length, 46–55 mm in diameter (averaging 50 mm in a group of twenty eggs), and 65–103 grams (g) in weight (averaging 86 g in a group of 160 eggs). Our pythons' fertile clutches have ranged from one to eleven eggs, with an average number of almost seven fertile eggs per clutch (in twenty-two clutches). The eggs are large and white or off-white in color and typically adhered to each other. We incubate ball python eggs at 90° F, and the eggs hatch in fifty-three to sixty days, averaging fifty-seven days.

Ball python eggs can be easily "candled" to check for fertility. To do this, place a small flashlight against an egg in a darkened room. Fertile eggs have an overall pinkish glow, and small thin red blood vessels on the inside of the shell. Infertile eggs typically glow yellow, and blood vessels are not apparent.

The general maintenance and environmental requirements of incubating ball python eggs are similar to the requirement of eggs of larger python species. In order to hatch, they require high relative humidity, but not wet or damp conditions, and temperatures of 86–91° F.

You can allow females to brood their eggs until hatching in proper conditions: high humidity and cage temperatures of 86–88° F. The eggs must be on a dry surface.

We remove the eggs from the females and incubate them in slightly damp vermiculite at 90° F. We use 13-gallon plastic

Ball python eggs hatching.

trash cans as egg containers, covering each top with a pane of glass. We place 8 to 10 gallons of vermiculite in these egg containers, adding just enough water so that, once mixed, the vermiculite will just clump if squeezed in the hand. We then place the egg container in a thermostatically heated room regulated to maintain a constant 90° F. Alternatively, you can place large plastic storage containers inside the incubator. Do not overcrowd eggs—they should cover no more than 50 percent of the vermiculite surface. Bury eggs about a third of their width in the vermiculite. Many breeders now use vermiculite-perlite mix (equal parts).

Ball python eggs are fairly hardy and can be gently handled and examined without negative effects. One of the best ways to determine if the eggs are in the proper humid conditions is to weigh them. In dry conditions, python eggs lose weight, and in wet conditions, they gain weight. We have seen python eggs hatch with weights 20 percent to 100 percent different from when they began. At either of those extremes, however, there is a high mortality rate. Ball python eggs seem to fare best with a weight gain of 10 to 40 percent during incubation.

Ball python eggs usually dimple about two weeks before hatching. During the last week of incubation, the shells become increasingly thin and pliable. Three or four days before hatching, the eggs begin to lose their adhesiveness and are easily separated.

A hatchling ball python with head just emerging from shell. Note the egg tooth at the tip of the snout.

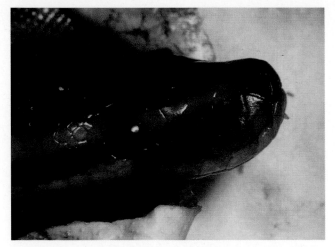

When hatching, a baby ball python slits several openings in the shell with its egg tooth, and then pokes its head out of the egg. At this time, a hatching ball python usually has a large amount of yolk outside its body and is still connected to its umbilicus by large blood vessels. This yolk is quickly absorbed into its body, after which time its umbilicus closes. The hatching ball python usually does not leave the egg until this process is completed, a period of twenty-four to thirty-six hours after it slits the egg. As soon as hatchlings emerge from the shell, transfer them to a clean enclosure with adequate heat, shelter, and water, and a relatively high ambient humidity.

# CHAPTER 8

# DISEASES AND DISORDERS

By Roger Klingenberg, DVM

Wild-caught and imported ball pythons are more dramatically affected by the stresses of captivity than are most other wild imports. These secretive and gentle snakes appear to be overwhelmed by the captive conditions in which other reptiles readily flourish. The stress of captivity alters the hormonal secretions that affect many of their day-to-day physiological functions and behaviors. Of the affected physiological processes, perhaps the most important is the suppression of the immune system. Current veterinary knowledge places great emphasis on supporting the immune system of these reptiles, both to prevent medical problems and to augment treatment when they do arise.

## Providing Heat

The easiest and most important way to support the immune system of a ball python is to provide a thermal gradient that reaches the upper range of the optimal temperature zone. Numerous studies have demonstrated that reptiles with access to such thermal gradients produce a better-coordinated immune response—including better antibody production, better cellular mobilization, and better suppression of pathogens. Reptiles kept in such a manner can create a "behavioral fever" by selecting warm areas when they are ill. In addition, certain antibiotics (for example, amikacin) administered at these higher temperatures performed better because of improved drug absorption and lower bacterial resistance. The safety of these antibiotics also improved at higher temperatures because they are more rapidly and efficiently eliminated from the body. For specific heating instructions, see Housing and Maintenance.

## Correcting Dehydration

The second most important means of supporting a ball python's immune system is to provide adequate hydration. Sick ball pythons are usually dehydrated as a result of fluid and electrolyte shifts in the body, and a mere dish of water is unlikely to correct these deficits. You can recognize a dehydrated snake by its loss of elasticity, which appears as wrinkles running laterally down the body (see Fig. 1). In more advanced cases of dehydration, the eyes have a sunken appearance.

A simple way to correct dehydration is to administer Gatorade or Pedialyte by means of a gastric tube. Both liquids offer easily absorbed fluids, electrolytes, amino acids,

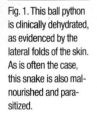

Fig. 1. This ball python is clinically dehydrated, as evidenced by the lateral folds of the skin. As is often the case, this snake is also malnourished and parasitized.

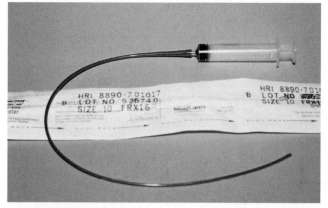

Fig. 2. These rubber tubes are trimmed at their flared ends so as to adapt to the tip of a syringe. The tubes are soft and atraumatic, yet rigid enough to allow passage.

and sugars. I prefer to use Sovereign red rubber tubes whose ends have been cut to adapt to a syringe for this purpose (see Fig. 2). Administer the fluids at the rate of 10–20 milliliters (ml) per kilogram (kg) of body weight of the snake every twenty-four to forty-eight hours, as needed. This method is illustrated in Fig. 3-6. Address dehydration before you address other nutritional needs.

## Nutritional Supplementation

Very thin, ill ball pythons that are not feeding require nutritional supplementation. I use an alimentary diet (a/d) or a homemade force-feed mix. Alimentary diets are syringeable food, available from veterinarians, that provide

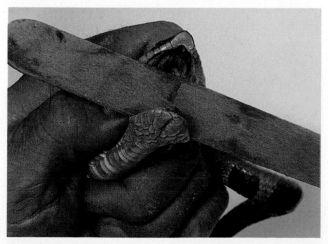

Fig. 3. Open the ball python's mouth to expose all internal structures and to allow the passage of a rubber tube.

Fig. 4. Use a ball point pen or long-handled cotton swab to open the mouth. It is important to use a gag that is minimally traumatic to the teeth and oral tissues.

an ideal combination of nutrients, vitamins, minerals, and electrolytes to prevent further tissue damage. Feed a proper alimentary diet at a rate of 1 ounce (30 ml) per kg of body weight every seven to twenty-one days, as needed. Mildly dehydrated snakes can have the a/d mixed at a one-to-one ratio with Lactated Ringers solution, Gatorade, or Pedialyte. Feed extremely emaciated animals every seven to ten days initially, and every twenty-one days once their condition is stable. Although a ball python could be nutritionally maintained in this manner, the goal is to sustain the animal until it is sufficiently adapted to captivity or healthy enough to start feeding on its own. Many experienced herpetoculturists refuse to force-feed ball pythons, for fear of causing them additional stress. I agree that ball pythons with good body mass and no serious ailments do not need to be force-fed. It is vital, however, for an emaciated and ill ball python to receive basic sustenance.

## Homemade Force-Feed Mix

1 jar pureed chicken baby food (2.5 oz.)
Equal parts Gatorade or Pedialyte
1/4 teaspoon vegetable oil
1 Tums tablet, crushed (for calcium)

Mix all ingredients well, and feed 1 ounce (30 ml) per kg every seven to 21 days as needed.

Fig. 5. Introduce the rubber tube through the center of the speculum and advance it against the roof of the mouth and down into the esophagus. Lubricating the tube with water or a small amount of alimentary diet allows for an easier passage.

Fig. 6. Advance the tube until only a few inches remain. Using the syringe containing the feeding formula (which is attached to the trimmed end of the catheter), administer the mixture slowly but steadily for a minute. If reflux of the mixture is seen, immediately remove the catheter and the gag and allow the snake to swallow.

## Ball Python Health Trouble-Shooting Chart

| Anatomical Region | Symptoms | Common Cause | Treatment |
|---|---|---|---|
| Eyes | Opaque eye(s); film on eye(s) | Retained eye cap | Increase humidity by light misting. Apply artificial tear (the type used to moisten your eyes) ointment to the eyes twice daily until loosened. Do not force loosening . |
| | Enlarged and bulging eye(s) | Infected eye; glaucoma; trauma | See a veterinarian. This ailment requires professional diagnosis and likely needs topical and systemic medications. |
| | Rim of eye elevated; puffy appearance | Mite infestation of postorbital space | Apply artificial tear ointment daily to suffocate mites. You can also move a small sexing probe gently around the postorbital space to mechanically eliminate the mites. General mite treatment is also recommended. |
| Nostrils | Occluded (plugged); open-mouth breathing | Retained shed skin; dried secretions from respiratory infections | For retained shed, apply artificial tear ointment (as with retained eye cap) until section loosens and then mechanically remove it. Watch for signs of respiratory disease. |
| Mouth | Mild distortion; hemorrhage spots; viscous secretions or caseous pus; excess salivation | Infectious stomatitis (mouth rot); infected tooth | Increase heat. Requires gentle surgical removal of loose tissues with Betadine solution, or peroxide. In all but the mildest cases, see veterinarian for systemic antibiotics. In case of infected teeth, simply pull tooth and clean mouth with aforementioned disinfectants. If the problem subsists, see a veterinarian. |
| Throat | Distended or inflated throat; bulging underneath | Respiratory infection | Increase heat. Make sure animal is not in respiratory distress. In all but the mildest cases, see a veterinarian. |
| Glottis and Trachea | Frothy saliva; open-mouth breathing; elevated head; clicking, popping, or wheezing | Respiratory infection | Increase heat. Make sure animal is not in respiratory distress. In all but the mildest cases, see a veterinarian. |

## Ball Python Health Trouble-Shooting Chart, Cont.

| Anatomical Region | Symptoms | Common Cause | Treatment |
|---|---|---|---|
| **Glottis and Trachea Cont.** | Noises | | Antibiotics and drying agents. Occasionally will need nebulization. |
| **Neurological System** | Inappropriate tongue flicking; jerky movements; lying on side or back; "gazing" | Meningitis; encephalitis, sometimes called "star gazing;" also caused by temperatures in excess of 100° for more than a few hours, viruses, tumors, trauma and (rarely) amoebic protozoans; almost all cases are caused by bacterial infection. | See veterinarian for diagnostic information and typical systemic antibiotic and steroid anti-inflammatory therapy. Metronidazole (Flagyl) is used successfully in some cases. |
| **Skin** | Excess dried skin, with edges that are peeled up but will not come off | Retained shed | Increase humidity by frequent misting. If unsuccessful, soak your animal in a 10-gallon aquarium with moistened bath towels and a loose cover to maintain high humidity. Short-duration soaks may only leave skin drier. |
| | Defined areas of dry, shrunken scales | Bacterial dermatitis, usually mistaken for fungus; check for localized areas of mites | Use a newspaper substrate while treating. Apply antibiotic ointment once daily for two to three weeks. Use Betadine ointment if fungus is suspected. If unresponsive, see a veterinarian. |
| | Scales with reddish color on belly; brown crumpled scales; ulcerated areas | Necrotic dermatitis (scale rot) | Increase temperature. Use newspaper for substrate. Apply antibiotic ointment once daily for two to three weeks. In all but the mildest cases, see a veterinarian. |
| | Elevated scales with small protuberances | Ticks | Pull out ticks by firmly grasping them with tweezers and pulling. Apply antibiotic ointment once daily for seven days. If infected, see a veterinarian. Watch for more ticks. |

## Ball Python Health Trouble-Shooting Chart, Cont.

| Anatomical Region | Symptoms | Common Cause | Treatment |
|---|---|---|---|
| **Skin, Cont.** | Soft, fluctuant masses | Aberrant, migrating tapeworms | Lance the area between scales (1/8 inch) and gently remove worms with a needle or tweezers. Flush area with Nolvasan, Betadine, or peroxide, and apply antibiotic ointment once daily for five to seven days. Treat the snake for tapeworms. |
| | Firm skin masses | Abscesses; cysts; granulomas; tumors | See a veterinarian for diagnosis and a treatment plan. |
| **Body** | Not gaining weight despite eating well | Parasitism | Have a fecal sample analyzed or any passed parasites examined. If parasites are present, see "Parasitism." |
| | Rear third of body distended; not eating | If female, likely gravid; if male, suspect severe constipation with possible intestine rupture | For gravid females, see Captive Reproduction. For suspected constipation, see "Gastrointestinal Disorders" and consult a veterinarian. |
| | Firm mass(es) within the body | Uric acid stones; retained fecal masses; retained eggs | If you suspect uric acid stones or fecal masses, try soaking the snake in tepid water to encourage defecation. If this produces no results, see a veterinarian for possible X-rays. |
| **Gastrointestinal System** | Bloody, mucus-laden; very rancid feces | Parasitism; gastroenteritis (usually bacterial) | Have a fecal evaluation performed. If no parasites are seen, a fecal culture and antibiotic may be needed. |
| | Regurgitation | Gastroenteritis: parasites; protozoans; bacteria; inadequate heat for digestion; foreign bodies | Withhold food for a few days, but make sure the snake is hydrated and warm. Resume feedings, giving small food items infrequently. Palpate for foreign bodies (retained skulls, uric acid balls masses, etc.). Consider having an exam performed by a veterinarian. One dose of metronidazole at 25–40 mg/kg will often clear mild bacterial and protozoal cases. Do not handle for at least forty-eight hours after feeding. |

The proper way to inject a ball python. Because snakes have a renal portal system, they should be injected in the anterior (front) third of their bodies.

## Diagnosing the Problem

By supporting the immune system with an appropriate temperature gradient, correcting dehydration, and providing nutritional supplementation, the following disorders and diseases are much easier to manage.

## Parasitism

Although parasites are fairly uncommon in captive-born ball pythons, they are the rule rather than the exception in wild-caught imports. At one time in my veterinary practice, three hundred consecutive ball pythons I examined had at least one internal parasite, and most of them had

One species of tick is common in imported ball pythons; its life cycle is somehow tied to the life cycle of these snakes. Following egg-laying, paired ticks will migrate from the female ball python to the eggs.

multiple parasites. Judging by fecal tests performed on several hundred ball pythons, I estimate more than 95 percent of wild-caught specimens harbor internal parasites and nearly 40 percent host external parasites (primarily ticks).

In order for your snake to live a healthy, long life, it is imperative that these parasites are eliminated. The following drugs and doses listed below proved to be very safe and effective in the treatment of several hundred ball pythons:

**Fenbendazole (Panacur):** dosed at 25 mg per kg once and orally administered every seven to ten days for at least three treatments, usually eliminates nematode parasites (such as roundworms and hookworms). I do not use ivermectin (Ivomec), which is also effective against nematode parasites, because of the rare chance of neurological effects.

**Praziquantel (Droncit):** dosed at 5–8 mg per kg and either orally administered or injected, is effective against cestodes (tapeworms) and some trematodes (flukes).

**Sulfadimethoxine (Albon):** is effective for coccidia when dosed at 50 mg per kg and administered orally once daily for three days, then, after three days off the medication, administered for another three days.

**Metronidazole (Flagyl):** can be used to treat flagellates when administered orally in doses ranging from 25 to 40 mg per kg. Repeat this dose in three days if needed.

Remove ticks with tweezers and treat the wound with a topical antibiotic ointment daily for a week. Because ticks can transmit bacterial diseases while feeding on the host, systemic antibiotics are often necessary.

Mites can be treated with No-Pest Strips (impregnated with 2.2 dichlorovinyl dimethyl phosphate), ivermectin spray, or pyrethroid spray. In individual cases, place a small piece of No-Pest Strip inside a jar (with holes punched in the lid) in the cage for three to four hours, two to three times weekly for three weeks. In larger collections, liberally spray a diluted ivermectin spray (10 mg spray to 1 quart water) in the cage and on the animal every four to five days, as needed. Although I don't use ivermectin for internal nematode parasites, this concentration of ivermectin has not caused any problems to date. Remove your snake's water dish while the pest strip is present and until the spray is dry. Only use No-Pest Strips in cages with good ventilation. I have had the best results using the ivermectin spray on infected animals and in their cage, and using a pyrethroid-based spray with residual action outside the cage and on shelves. You can use ivermectin spray outside the cage and on shelves, but the duration of its effectiveness is unknown. Thoroughly clean your snake's cage and eliminate all noncleanable hiding materials before attempting any of these methods, otherwise they will not succeed.

## Skin Infections

Ball pythons tend to have a high incidence of skin problems, which are often related to external parasites. Necrotizing dermatitis, or "scale rot," is common as well, and signs of infection require aggressive treatment. The earliest sign of infection is evidence of bleeding beneath the belly scales, which gives the scales a red or pink tint. While this is a normal pigment change in some snakes (boa constrictors, for example), it is not normal in ball pythons.

To help prevent possible problems, provide your snake with a water dish just large enough to use for drinking but not large enough for soaking. Some ball pythons use large dishes to hide, and consequently get waterlogged. Excessive soaking may also indicate the presence of mites, so you should search for dead mites in the bottom of any dishes used for soaking.

Excessive moisture can predispose snakes to skin problems, but external parasites and the local manifestation of a severe septicemia are more common causes. The skin seems to be a weak organ system in ball pythons and is affected by many common disorders.

## Gastrointestinal Disorders

Many owners find that their newly purchased import suffers from regurgitation and/or the production of copious mucus-laden, blood-tinged, or excessively fetid stools. Gastroenteritis, an inflammation of the gastrointestinal lining, is generally caused by internal parasites, protozoans, bacterial infections, or poor husbandry techniques. Internal parasites and protozoans can be found through a fecal examination and are easily treated with appropriate medications. Inadequate heating can cause immune suppression and prevent the normal digestion of foodstuffs in the gastrointestinal tract. Excessive handling within two to three days of feeding may cause regurgitation in nervous ball pythons.

Bacterial infections are common, perhaps because opportunistic bacteria quickly take advantage of a weakened host. To maintain normal intestinal bacterial flora, ball pythons require regular feeding and elimination. Most imported ball pythons are undernourished and dehydrated, conditions that contribute to the alteration of their normal intestinal bacterial flora, thereby allowing other bacteria to proliferate. These snakes are usually exposed to dozens of other snakes, and, therefore, to contagious parasitic, bacterial, and even viral pathogens. For very mild cases, orally administer metronidazole at 25–40 mg per kg given as a single dose or on the first and third days. Metronidazole is used most often as an antiprotozoan drug, but it is also an excellent gastrointestinal antibiotic, especially for hard-to-detect anaerobic bacteria. In refractory cases, your veterinarian may need to perform a fecal culture to identify the causative agent and to give antibiotics.

When dealing with regurgitation or diarrhea, it is also important to withhold foods during treatment in order to allow the intestinal lining to heal. Fluid therapy (as previously described) is indicated unless this also causes regurgitation. If the python appears to be doing well after treatment, initially offer very small and infrequent meals. For a ball python weighing 1 kg, this meal would consist of a pinkie rat or a very small mouse once every seven to ten days. Once the snake is eating and eliminating normally, gradually build up its feeding regimen to normal amounts over the course of two to three weeks. Although it may seem difficult to overfeed a ball python, excessive feeding can create maldigestion and gastrointestinal irritation.

# RESOURCES

Cansdale, G.S. 1961 (reprinted 1973): *West African Snakes.* Longman Group Ltd., London. 74 pp.

Carter, R. 1990: "Captive Propagation of the Ball Python." *The Monitor,* Vol. II, #3.

Conant, R. 1993: "The Oldest Snake." *Bulletin of the Chicago Herpetological Society.* Vol. 28, #4, pp. 77-78.

Frye, F.L. 1981: *Biomedical and Surgical Aspects of Captive Reptile Husbandry.* Veterinary Medicine Publishing Co. Kansas.

Peterson, K. 1993: "Husbandry and Breeding of Ball Pythons." *The Vivarium* (Vol.5 No.1 1993).

Pitman, C.R.S. 1974: *A Guide to the Snakes of Uganda* (Revised edition). Wheldon and Wesley, Codicote, 290 pp.

Ross, R.A. 1979: *The Python Breeding Manual.* Institute for Herpetological Research.

Spawls, S. 1989: "Some Notes and Reminiscences on the Royal Python, *Python regius* in Ghana and elsewhere." *Snake Keeper,* Vol. 3, No. 3, pp. 11-1

# INDEX

## A
abscesses, 78
acclimation, 13–14, 16, 23
adult pythons: beginning herpetoculturists and, 8–9; feeding, 25–30, 73–75; handling, 14, 23, 24, 25, 60; parasites in, 5, 8, 13, 22, 79–80; sexing, 60; size of, 7; subadults, 23–25
adult pythons, health of: dehydration, 72–73, 74; fasting, 22, 28–29; gastrointestinal disorders, 78, 81–82; likely diseases, 8; selecting for, 9–11; skin disorders, 77–78, 81; stool checks, 13, 78, 82
albino morphs: albinism as recessive trait, 35, 37; lavender albino, 52; results of breeding, 37, 38–39; T-negative, 45; T-positive, 46–47
alimentary diet, 73–75
amelanism. See albino morphs
aspen shavings, how to use, 16–17
axanthic morph, 35, 36

## B
bacterial dermatitis, 77
bacterial infections, 82
ball pythons: benefits of owning, 4; general information, 6–7; problems associated with owning, 5, 8. See also adult pythons; females; hatchlings
Barker, Dave and Tracy, 50
base morphs: albino (See albino morphs); axanthic, 35, 36, 47; black pastel, 54; caramel, 46–47; cinnamon pastel, 40, 54; clown, 50–51; combinations of, 36–37; fire, 54; ghost, 45–46; lavender albino, 52; meaning of, 42–43; Mojave, 52; overview, 44; pastel jungle, 39, 40, 48; piebald, 35–39, 42, 48–49; pinstripe, 52–53; platinum, 53; spider, 39, 51; woma tiger, 49; yellowbelly, 39, 40, 49–50
belly area, signs of infection on, 10
black pastel morph, 54
black-eyed leucistic morph, 56
blue-eyed leucistic morph, 41, 56
breeding. See captive reproduction
bumble bee morph, 55–56

## C
captive reproduction: combat between

males, 65–66; copulation, 65, 66; eggs, 68–69; environmental conditions and feeding, 64–65; ovulation and egg laying, 66–68; photoperiod and, 18–19; sexing, 59–61; sexual maturity, 61–62; unpredictable results, 40–41. See also reproductive cycle
captive-bred hatchlings: beginning herpetoculturists and, 8; feeding, 23–25; need for, 5
caramel morph, 46–47
cedar shavings, caveat about, 16
cinnamon pastel morph, 40, 54
cloacal opening: healthy appearance of, 10–11; sexing adults, 60; spurs, 59
clown morph, 50–51
codominant traits, 39–40
coiling, 22, 23
Conant, Roger, 7
constipation, 78
cysts, 78

## D
defensive reactions: coiling, 22, 23; to force-feeding, 29; to rodents entering shelter, 27
dehydration, 72–73, 74
dermatitis, 77
designer morphs: black-eyed leucistic, 56; blue-eyed leucistic, 41, 56; bumble bee, 55–56; high gold, 36; high white piebald, 36; high yellow albino, 6, 34; ivory, 40, 50, 56; lavender albino piebald, 57; overview, 42–43, 54–55; pewter, 57; pewter pastel, 40, 41; snowball, 56; spinner, 56; super cinnamon, 57; super pastel jungle, 40, 55; super pastel spider, 56; super yellowbelly, 40, 50, 56; wide-striped, 24; wild, 7, 43–44
diseases and disorders: checking for, 9–11; dehydration, 72–73, 74; immune system support, 71–72; in imported adults, 8. See also parasitism
double hets, 38

## E
eggs: egg laying and brooding, 67–68; female behavior in the wild, 26; incubating, 20, 68–69; mother-to-egg weight comparison, 68; retained, 78
encephalitis, 77
enclosures: avoiding dampness, 31; gastroenteritis from inadequate, 82; heating, 17–18, 19–20, 71–72; lighting, 18–19; plastic shoe boxes as, 66; shelters for, 20–21, 26–27; size of, 15; suitable pens, 15, 16, 17, 18
enteric diseases, 8

# ABOUT THE AUTHORS

**Philippe de Vosjoli** is the highly acclaimed author of the best-selling reptile care books, The Herpetocultural Library™ series. His work in the field of herpetoculture has been recognized nationally and internationally for establishing high standards for amphibian and reptile care. His books, articles, and other writings have been praised and recommended by numerous herpetological societies, veterinarians, and other experts in the field. Philippe de Vosjoli was also the cofounder and president of The American Federation of Herpetoculturists and was given the Josef Laszlo Memorial Award in 1995 for excellence in herpetoculture and his contribution to the advancement of the field.

**Roger Klingenberg**, DVM, is a graduate of Colorado State University Veterinary School. He is a well-known author, speaker, and researcher on herpetoculture and herpetological medicine and surgery and has authored dozens of papers, articles, and text chapters on these topics. He is the author of *Understanding Reptile Parasites*, the popular bestseller in herpetological medicine. He is the founder, owner, and senior veterinarian of a busy veterinary practice that serves small and exotic pets, and is an active member of the Association of Amphibian and Reptile Veterinarians. Dr. Klingenberg is probably best known for his collaborations with Philippe de Vosjoli, having co-authored several texts including *The Box Turtle Manual, The Boa Constrictor Manual,* and several others.

**David Barker and Tracy Barker** are graduate biologists with more than forty years of combined experience with amphibians and reptiles. Thy both have expansive herpetological backgrounds including training and work in zoo herpetological collections, museum collections, and field research. They are the authors of *Pythons of the World: Australia*, an authoritative and highly awaited reference on these fascinating snakes. David and Tracy own Vida Preciosa International, Inc., the largest and most diverse collection of pythons in the world.

**Alan Bosch**, a native of New Orleans, Louisiana, had his first experience with reptiles at eight years old when he captured a ring-necked snake (*Diadophis punctuas*), igniting his lifelong passion for herpetology. He studied at the University of Wyoming under the famed Wyoming herpetologist Dr. George T. Baxter, and in 1979 graduated with a BS in Wildlife Management. In 1996, Alan began a full-time career breeding and selling reptiles through his business, Alan Bosch Reptiles. As president of the Coastal Carolina Herpetocultural Society, Alan has been able to reinforce the ideals of reptile and amphibian collecting and captive maintenance as well as spearhead many local field trips and educational sessions. Contact Alan at http://www.alanboschreptiles.com.